# Shopping

# The Ultimate Guide on How to Overcome Compulsive Buying and Spending

**Copyright 2015 by Caesar Lincoln - All rights reserved.**

This document is geared towards providing exact and reliable information in regards to the topic and issue covered. The publication is sold with the idea that the publisher is not required to render accounting, officially permitted, or otherwise, qualified services. If advice is necessary, legal or professional, a practiced individual in the profession should be ordered.

In no way is it legal to reproduce, duplicate, or transmit any part of this document in either electronic means or in printed format. Recording of this publication is strictly prohibited, and any storage of this document is not allowed, unless with written permission from the publisher. All rights reserved.

The information provided herein is stated to be truthful and consistent, in that any liability, in terms of inattention or otherwise, by any usage or abuse of any policies, processes, or directions contained within is the solitary and utter responsibility of the recipient reader. Under no circumstances will any legal responsibility or blame be held against the publisher for any reparation, damages, or monetary loss due to the information herein, either directly or indirectly.

The information herein is offered for informational purposes solely and is universal as so. The presentation of the information is without contract or any type of guarantee assurance.

The trademarks that are used are without any consent, and the publication of the trademark is without permission or backing by the trademark owner. All trademarks and brands within this book are for clarifying purposes only and are owned by the owners themselves, not affiliated with this document.

# Table of Contents

Introduction

Chapter 1: Understanding Addiction

Chapter 2: Diagnosing a Victim of Shopping Addiction

Chapter 3: Telltale Signs & Symptoms of Shopping Addiction

Chapter 4: The Psychology of Overcoming Shopping Addiction

Chapter 5: Medication & Therapy

Chapter 6: The "Conscious" Shopper

Chapter 7: Happy and Content - That's All That Matters

Conclusion

# Introduction

The pages in this short book were developed through years of experiences that I have gone through, as well as what has been proven to work for others that I have talked to and have researched. I also want to congratulate you for taking the time to understand your own shopping addiction and how you can overcome it.

I can guarantee that you will find this book useful if you make sure to implement what you learn in the following pages. The important thing is that you IMPLEMENT what you learn; a shopping addiction is not conquered overnight, but the important thing to remember is that it is definitely possible for you to overcome it. What I am giving you is the information that will enable you to understand your own mind, how shopping addictions negatively affect those around you, and the steps you will need to make that journey.

Many people experience shopping addictions and aren't really aware of the signs and symptoms that are going on. There is a difference between casually shopping recreationally and unconsciously feeling the need to spend money in order to fill a deeper need. As you go through these pages, you'll get a better understanding of what shopping addiction really is, the signs and symptoms of someone who has a shopping addiction, and you will learn several ways that you can overcome it. We will dive into what is going on in your mind, how your body reacts to your triggers, how your early childhood can influence the rest of your life, and what work is required of you to get past the roadblocks you have.

I recommend that you take notes while you are reading this book. This will ensure that you get the most out of the information in here. I want you to look over the notes of this book, even after you've finished reading it, because the notes will help you pinpoint exactly what you need to implement, and by writing things down, you will be able to recall specifics and how to handle certain situations when they arise. I want you to feel that you made a purchase that is worth your money.

Lastly, remember that everything in this book has been compiled through research, my own experiences, and the experiences of others, so feel free to question what you have read in this book. I encourage you to do your own research on the things that you want to look deeper into. The more you understand about your own mind and habits, the better off you'll be. To overcome a shopping addiction in your life, it will take some work on your part, but you CAN do it! So remember to read with confidence and an open mind!

# Chapter 1:

# Understanding Addiction

*"To know what is wrong, one must first know what is right."*

We start our journey by answering this all-important question: What is addiction? At first, you might think an addiction is simply an attachment or over-indulgence in something. However, you might not know there is more to addiction than just dependence. Most psychologists, today, categorize addiction as a form of mental handicap. It is, in a way, a psychological problem that sometimes affects people unconsciously.

No matter what form of addiction a person has, there is always an opportunity to make a change. It is from the understanding of what addiction is and how it is triggered in a person's mentality that the cure may be found. So, if you want to change your life or the life of others from being an addict, then the first thing we should do is understand from where the triggers are coming.

# Shopping Addiction 101

There are many types of addictions, and one of them is *shopping addiction*; sometimes it also called *oniomania, compulsive buying disorder,* or *compulsive spending disorder*. People who have this addiction cannot control how they spend money, and quite often, they will compulsively buy and spend for a random item; they will do this with little regard to the possible consequences.

Shopping addiction was introduced to the public for the first time in the 1920s; it was discussed in the journals of a well-respected psychologist, named Emil Kraepelin. According to the psychologist, this disorder was so profound that it was included in early psychiatric textbooks. However, the interest regarding this type of behavior waned through the years.

Today, oniomania is considered a huge problem, and many agree that such a disorder is hard to diagnose. People with shopping addictions often encounter financial problems, as their spending is not managed accordingly. Aside from that, shopping addicts are also prone to dealing with *scammers, opportunists, ruined relationships*, and might even end up with *bad credit, buried in debt*, and basically, stuck in a poor financial state.

Moreover, the cases of shopping addiction have increased, especially since *online shopping* entered the picture. With a stable internet connection, money in your bank account, and a mere willingness to buy stuff, you can begin to shop – and shop until you drop. Now, with shopping as a virtually effortless activity, it has become more difficult to fight the underlying cause of the problem.

## Shopping Addiction & Its Types

Usually, it's easy to generalize shopping addiction, according to the stereotype. People who shop more frequently than the rest are instantly labeled as shopping addicts, regardless of the facts that contribute to the particular behavior.

To have a thorough understanding of shopping addiction, it's best to be familiar with its types. Especially if you are interested in curing the problem, a closer inspection is a great way to start. Let's look at the common types of shopping addiction:

## Bargain Shopping Addiction

This type of addiction afflicts the "religious" shoppers. Bargain shopaholics religiously jot down the names of the stores that offer bargains, clearances, and discounts, then they make sure they show up at the date of the sale to hoard less-costly stuff.

"It's economic", they say, despite not exactly having a use for the particular items on sale. If you're the kind who hunts for bargains, you may fall into this category.

# Bulimic Shopping Addiction

Bulimic shopaholics are usually indecisive and fickle-minded. Their pattern of spending money is purchasing an item, over-thinking whether an item is a need or a want, and returning it, whether or not they get a refund. As victims to the compulsive behavior, they do this repeatedly.

Aside from having to deal with needless problems on their own, they bring inconvenience to other parties involved; it is time-consuming and can be downright irritating to some sellers.

# Co-Dependent Shopping Addiction

Shopping for gifts (to give to other people) may seem selfless and kind; if done inappropriately, however, it may mean the shopper is a co-dependent shopaholic. He/she craves attention and tries to get it by buying things for others to make them happy, despite the fact that they're not exactly unhappy.

The act of giving, in this case, is seen as needless and selfish, especially since it is self-damaging. Giving presents is one thing; shopping for them to satisfy a personal need is another.

## Collective Shopping Addiction

Collective shopping addiction describes an obsession with a particular item; if an item comes in a set (e.g. various colors, different sizes, and different brands), a collective shopping addict needs to purchase the entire set.

For instance, if he/she fancies a specific design of jeans, he/she won't hold back from getting as many versions of it as he/she can. Possible budget concerns won't stand in this person's way; neither will practicality.

# Retail Therapy Shopping Addiction

Although some people believe it is a form of treatment or reward, retail therapy shopping can actually be a problem. Instead of being an adaptive behavior, it becomes a maladaptive one. If you turn to it too often, and it is injuring your financial health, you're probably in need of help.

Although shopping can be a way to improve one's mood, it can be troubling if an important issue is ignored in favor of shopping. For example, if you insist on shopping, despite not having enough money in your account to purchase stuff, it's an apparent sign that the *therapeutic effects* of shopping aren't working; it has activated another problem, instead.

## Pretentious Shopping Addiction

If you're the shopper who dwells on the idea of being perceived as rich, you might be a pretentious shopaholic. Your target items are the expensive ones, and you find pleasure in other people knowing you can afford them.

Although there's nothing wrong with how you prefer to spend your own money, the problem can hurt you financially in the long run. Rather than saving even just a fraction of your salary, you disregard the need to be practical and use it all to buy costly stuff, to impress others.

# Thrill-Seeking Shopping Addiction

A thrill-seeking shopping addict is someone who is focused on spending money for the excitement of the act. The person gains a sense of validation if he/she has control over the big amount he/she squanders away.

The person's agenda is on using money; it has nothing to do with the item itself. Aside from giving the person a thrill, a pricey item rewards him/her with a feeling of superiority.

# Trophy Shopping Addiction

Trophy shopping addiction is the type of shopping addiction that revolves around buying the most attractive items. If you are a trophy shopping addict, it wouldn't matter whether or not the items have a particular use; what matters is they make you feel giddy the instant you lay eyes on them.

And, regardless of a particular item's price, whether $2 or $5,000, the urge to take it to the counter and bring it home for the mere reason that it looks nice will be irresistible. Only once the item(s) is in your possession, will you get your high and be satisfied.

# Shopping Spree vs. Shopping Addiction

According to a study conducted by Stanford University's psychology department, sometimes, someone who is simply on a *shopping spree* is mistaken by others to be a shopping addict.

Especially if the person is spotted buying too many items, he/she is immediately thought to be afflicted with addiction, and he/she needs intervention for the management of the spending habit before it exacerbates. If the person has justifiable reasons (e.g. received a huge sum and in the process of collecting holiday gifts), he/she may just be on a one-time roll.

Moreover, many people, especially those with less disposable income, wait to do their shopping on large sales days and purchase in bulk to save money.

## What Exactly Are You Shopping for?

Being aware of your personal shopping agenda is the first step to the treatment of your addiction. Are you targeting a particular item? Do you want to buy something, because you can afford it now? Or, do you simply want to spend money for the fun of it?

Essentially, find out if you can control your actions. By dwelling on the real reason you shop compulsively, you can often get to the bottom of whether or not there is a need to modify your behavior, and ultimately, you learn to face the real problem.

# Reasons for Shopping Addiction

Most psychologists agree that oniomania is a manifestation of unfulfilled wants during the early years of a person's life, especially during childhood. In this theory, people who had a hard life as children are more prone to this kind of behavior. This is aggravated when these same people now have the means to spend on every single item they want. A large portion of the shopping addicts around the world cite negative childhood experiences as a major factor in the forming of compulsive shopping and spending behaviors.

*Anxiety, nervousness, depression, and repressed feelings of emptiness* can also be let loose by excessive shopping. Many compulsive shoppers admit their reasons for indulging in shopping sprees are to release stress and find comfort in what they buy. Even if they refuse to admit it, they know they are troubled emotionally. The behavior serves as a temporary, but worthwhile, solution in their eyes. They prefer to keep their minds occupied with the "high" they get in spending money; for a moment, they experience euphoria, and for them, that's sufficient.

We must understand that people engaging in this kind of behavior are often sufferers as well, though they might not perceive it as so. That is why our first plan to help people overcome their shopping addiction is to educate them about their problem and show them they need help in that area of their life. If the support system around the addict fails to realize, at least, part of the cause to the addiction was out of the person's control, it makes it harder to sympathize and move forward with the process of overcoming it.

As odd as it may sound, many shopping addicts are actually unaware of the trouble their compulsive habits are causing. It is usually when a close friend or family member confronts them that they begin to notice the consequences of their actions. However, even with the consequences pointed out to them, without identifying the mental triggers, the compulsive behavior will continue.

# A Myth About Shopping Addiction

A common myth people believe about shopping addicts is that shopping addiction is only a *problem of the rich*; financial problems are unheard of without money. Well, this is not true. There are many people from all different socio-economic backgrounds who have to deal with shopping addiction.

This is because, generally, shopping addiction isn't diagnosed based on the types of things the person is buying or how much they are spending. It is based on the fact that a person is looking to the act of buying an item to fulfill a void in their own personal happiness.

## Chapter Recap:

Addiction is a psychological behavior, and many addictions are unconsciously performed, at least until they are pointed out by family members or close personal friends.

Oniomania is the medical term for shopaholism. It is often, though not always, the result of a bad child-parent relationship and repressed feelings of low self-esteem.

To help someone overcome shopping addiction, it is recommended to be familiar with the different types of shopping addiction; not all "frequent" shoppers are one and the same. If you dig deeper into the shopping addict's ways, you can develop a clearer grasp of their problem.

It is important to understand that, in order to help a compulsive spender, we must look at them as people who need help, not just as *inconsiderate or selfish people*. Although it is frustrating for the people involved in the life of a shopping addict, it is also important for them to understand that to overcome the addiction, it will take time, and a different mindset must be adopted.

The first step to overcoming this addiction is accepting the presence of this problem in one's life and to be willing to find solutions to change it.

# Chapter 2:

# Diagnosing a Victim of Shopping Addiction

In the first chapter, we focused on understanding what addiction is and how it applies to a shopping addict. We dissected the ways of an addict and the reasons behind the personality; he/she is someone who needs help, instead of being pre-judged. In this chapter, we will look into the common causes of shopping addiction - specifically.

# A Perk to Being a Shopping Addict

As with many addiction cases, the direct benefit of shopping addiction is the immediate gratifying experience you feel when you buy something you desire. If you buy things, then you feel happy in some way, and this happiness is what makes some people compulsive shoppers.

In such a situation, however, the goal of instant gratification is somewhat flawed; you are too occupied finding *a quick solution* that you end up ignoring a "bigger" problem. We must remember that spending money on shopping to feel happy is not bad; the bad thing is when we spend our money in a way that does not benefit our lives or the lives of others around us. Especially if excessive shopping is clearly hurting your financial condition, it becomes imperative to correct the behavior.

# The Five Common Causes

As mentioned in the previous chapter, shopping addiction is a problem that conceals another problem; generally, those with this particular addiction are troubled mentally. In an attempt to eliminate the inconvenience brought about by their illness, they rely on the gratification granted by spending money and purchasing items. The compulsive habit is merely a form of escape; it allows the shopping addict a chance to feel "lifted" from their current state.

We've looked at the common types of shopping addiction in Chapter 1. Let's now briefly look at the common causes:

# The Illusion of Control

Another thing that re-enforces the behavior of the shopping addict is the "*illusion of control*". When you buy things, in a way, you feel you are in control, and you can get what you want at any time. This feeling of control is very addictive to those who desire it, and sometimes, it fuels the desire for some to shop excessively.

Moreover, the illusion of control is often ignored; it is something that many shopping addicts have never really considered deeply, because they are not able to step away from their problem and look at it objectively. If you are around a shopping addict after a new purchase, it is not uncommon to see a big spike in attitude after the purchase of the new item.

# Following Trends

Many would say they are just being fashionable, following trends, catching on to fads, and any other related scenarios can be among the major causes of shopping addiction. The cultural background of a person will dictate the level of influence peer pressure has on him/her and how it can change the person's behavior. In some cases, people become shopping addicts because they constantly seek the approval of their peers.

These people are those who may consistently buy things, just for the sake of impressing friends or family members. The problem here is, if a person develops friendships based on *materialistic possessions*, those friendships are usually not authentic in the first place. It is almost as if the compulsive shopper is basing his/her self-image on the opinions of others, regardless of whether or not these people care about him/her.

# Childhood Deprivations

There are cases when people buy things because they didn't have such when they were young; especially during their childhood years, when their *material wishes* (e.g. bikes, huge water guns, and doll houses) were not given attention, they end up maximizing their financial capabilities as adults.

Deprived children often long for that day when they will have the means to get what they want, especially the things their parents or guardians were unable to provide for them. This repressed, unsatisfied need to get the desired things, tends to compound and, eventually, is released when the person has the chance to fulfill those desires.

## Outlet for Emotional Problems

Some people vent their frustration in activities, such as going to theaters, playing video games, eating out, and/or shopping. Some people regard shopping as an avenue to release emotional strains, which is not bad unless it becomes so frequent that it becomes an addiction.

This is a tricky one, because there is no real line for which emotional shopping becomes "bad". It is different for all people. For example, some forms of emotional outlets include gambling at casinos, betting on sporting events, or even going to gentlemen's clubs.

## Psychological Disorders

Those with shopping addiction are more likely to be diagnosed with psychological disorders (e.g. personality disorders, social phobia, depression, and social anxiety). These people are genuinely unable to resist the urge to buy things and may need serious psychological help.

However, as we'll cover in the following chapters, not all people who suffer from a shopping addiction need serious psychological help. Often, it can be overcome without long-term professional guidance, depending on how serious the person is about overcoming their problem and how severe and deep-rooted the problem is.

# The Importance of Knowing the Causes

As mentioned before, it is very important that we know what causes shopping addiction to correctly assess whether one is suffering from this behavior. According to research by students of Duke University, while there are about a tenth of men and women (in the US) who are shopping addicts, not all of them have the slightest clue they have a problem.

Now that we know the main causes of addiction and shopping addiction, specifically, we can start our assessment. We can now ask…

*Are you or is someone you know a shopping addict?*

## Chapter Recap:

Peer pressure is one of the major causes of shopping addiction, especially if the person is always trying to impress people they barely know. This behavior is often linked to low self-esteem and low self-worth.

Seeking to gain control and to feel in control at all times can push people to buy things compulsively.

Shopping addiction may be a manifestation of a deprived childhood, especially if the child grew up in an underprivileged household.

Shopping addiction may be caused by psychological disorders that affect emotional behavior. In these cases, professional psychological help is recommended.

# Chapter 3:

# Telltale Signs & Symptoms of Shopping Addiction

In this chapter, we begin our assessment; we address the issue discussed in a forum at Columbia University. Spotting a shopping addict can be easily accomplished with the help of a concerned peer; especially if the observant is familiar with the usual routines of the shopping addict, he/she can bring up the fact that there is a problem.

# The Seven Signs of Shopping Addiction

Just like a doctor who needs to diagnose the illness of his/her patients to provide the correct records and treatment, shopping addicts should also do a lifestyle diagnosis to check whether or not they have an addiction. The following are signs that may tell you whether you suffer from shopping addiction:

# Excessive Spending on Unimportant Things

It is important to make it clear that spending money on excess things is not inherently bad. However, if you are spending too much on things of lesser importance in the trade-off for more important things, then there is a clear-cut problem.

For example:

*Dave is a businessman, who happens to have a loving wife and two kids. Every payday, he buys things for his kids. He buys new toys, clothes, gifts of all sorts, and he also buys something for his wife. When he comes home, he gives these to his kids and wife and sleeps a happy man. The following morning, he wakes up, only to see late, unpaid bills on the table.*

In this scenario, Dave clearly has some kind of problem, as he is neglecting to allot money for paying the unpaid bills, because he is more focused on bringing joy to the other people in his life and spends excessively on buying things for them. If you or someone you know is like Dave, then there is, undoubtedly, a problem in mindset.

## Constant and Needless Buying

Many cases of shopping addiction involve people constantly buying things they don't really need. These are people who will buy clothes, shoes, kitchenware, and such, only to store and never actually use them.

It is important to know that most shopaholics buy things on impulse. They buy things because they like them, and they have the money or the means to purchase the items.

## Bouts of Sadness, Depression, and/or Anger

Having outlets for emotional strain is not bad; however, in some cases, it becomes an excuse for abuse. In the cases of some sufferers of shopping addiction, they find an emotional outlet in spending and shopping. There are instances where people will spend hundreds, even thousands, of dollars, just because they want to feel some type of comfort when they are down.

One must remember, there are more productive ways to vent steam, and spending excessively is not the most healthy way to resolve emotional strain.

# Shopping is ALWAYS the Solution

If a person has a headache, he/she ends up shopping. If a person is dealing with an unwanted load at work, he/she ends up shopping. If a person spent five hours arguing with a friend, he/she ends up shopping. For the shopper, a little amount of unwanted stress justifies this compulsive behavior. Instead of turning to healthier means, he/she prefers to shop.

# Embarrassment Regarding Purchased Items

Most compulsive buyers tend to be embarrassed about their spending habits and often hide their activities from family and friends. This type of behavior tends to break the trust between family members and friends, and may lead to misunderstandings.

Thousands of people suffer from emotional distress because of irksome disagreements that stem from shopping addiction. If you realize you are beginning to feel ashamed of your purchases or even trying to hide the fact that you purchased an item, it is time to evaluate why you are purchasing those items and how (if) they are actually benefitting your life.

## Overusing Credit Cards

Another common problem of shopaholics is having bad credit, due to overusing credit cards. Everyone must understand that credit cards are a convenient way to acquire things you need in an instant. However, this convenience is sadly abused, thus becoming the favorite spending method of people suffering from shopping addiction.

The convenience provided by using credit cards allows people to use their cards excessively without consciously keeping track of their spending, until they receive the bill.

In some cases, shopaholics prefer to use credit cards over paying for an item with cash, because they can avoid having to see the money leave their hand. A great method used to break the habit of compulsive buying is to start using cash instead of cards. If you feel you are going to go on a shopping spree, go to the local cash withdrawal or ATM machine and withdraw the cash first. This will force you to be much more conscious when you decide to fork over some hard-earned cash for an item.

# Unapologetic Damages to Meaningful Relationships

If asked about your shopping behavior, your response is a lie; since you know a sermon is probably forthcoming, you end up weaving a colorful, make-believe version of the issue. You don't acknowledge their concern for you. You insist that you know better, and you are not helping nurture your bond this way.

More importantly, instead of letting them help you, you are intentionally doing wrong. If dodging a sermon is more important to you than actually discussing the significance of the current situation, it's an implication that shopping trumps the relationships you have with others.

## Chapter Recap:

Shopaholics will often spend money on unnecessary things, rather than allotting money for the important obligations, such as home bills.

Shopaholics may constantly buy things they don't need and have no plan of actually using.

Shopaholics usually shop or spend when feeling down, depressed, and/or angry. Shopping serves as their outlet to vent these emotions.

Shopaholics may think the solution to virtually any personal dilemma is to go shopping.

Shopaholics can overuse their credit card, instead of saving and buying items with cash.

Shopping addiction can ruin meaningful relationships.

It is always important to be aware of the physical and mental symptoms of shopping addiction. This way, it becomes easier to help a friend.

# Chapter 4:

# The Psychology of Overcoming Shopping Addiction

Overcoming any type of addiction is not an easy thing to do. You can think of it like abruptly giving up your favorite TV show, suddenly putting an end to the usual 24-7 conversations with a significant other, or letting go of a favorite pet; sometimes, it can be even harder.

Freeing yourself from the bonds of addiction requires a lot of self-control and willpower. One must condition the mind to cope with the change and be willing to undergo drastic transformations in order to effectively overcome addiction. These are some of the things you should keep in mind when committing to the journey of full recovery.

## Acceptance + Appreciation

Acceptance of your shopping problem is a start; it is the first and most crucial step towards recovery. Unless you fully accept that your situation is not ideal in your mind and accept the fact that you need help, any chance of recovery will be for naught. Trying to overcome an addiction and being afraid to admit it cannot co-exist.

Therefore, accept the fact that you're a shopping addict – that you have a problem. It can be difficult to come to the harsh reality, but it's doable. After finding the courage to admit you're on a troubled road, it's time to adjust your perspective and appreciate the opportunity to improve. Tell yourself that you may have become someone whose nature is not easy to embrace, but it doesn't mean that the road is hopeless from that point forward.

# Reconciliation Is Key

Do you remember all of those people who told you that you have a spending problem, the people that you disregarded? Reconcile with them and acknowledge them for their concerns. Show them your appreciation and allow them to help you. Take note, a heavy load becomes light when many are sharing the weight.

This step, alone, will usually bring so much more positive energy towards overcoming the problem; not only will you have much more support in trying to overcome your addiction, but you will not feel as guilty anymore, because you aren't hiding your weakness.

Remember, reconciliation will help you overcome a mental problem, since it grants you peace of mind. Everyone has problems in life, and you never know what other people are going through. One of the best revelations you can have in your life is realizing every single person in the world has issues they deal with every day. By accepting this premise, you can effectively move forward and be more open with the people in your life.

# Yes, You Have a Shopping Addiction

Normally, people will feel ashamed after admitting to having an addiction, but try not to make this the case for you. Yes, having an addiction can be shameful, but you should be more proud than anything else, because, instead of just succumbing to it, you are standing up and trying hard to overcome it.

Remember, the first time you tell people about your issues will be the hardest for you, but learn to be brave. If you can just get over that initial hurdle, you will definitely be able to handle the rest.

# A Change of Lifestyle Is A Change of Heart

It is a wise idea to start changing habits in order to avoid the urge to shop. Adding productive hobbies can be a good start. Try fishing, jogging, swimming, or any kind of activity that doesn't involve spending money but, nevertheless, keeps your mind occupied.

Leaving the old and starting anew is a helpful remedy for edging out a shopping problem. It is amazing when people pick up a hobby they had been ignoring for the longest time, and because of it, they seem to become passionate about life again, and their previous problems seem like minuscule issues.

## Chapter Recap:

Acceptance is the first thing one should do to start overcoming shopping addiction. Remind yourself that, although you have a problem, you are still valuable.

Shopping addiction often alienates people, especially loved ones, which is why the next thing you should do is reconcile with them. If you've pushed them away, because they attempted to help, avoid letting the problem worsen. Say sorry and admit to your past actions and ask every person close to you for emotional support and help.

Start your new life with a clean slate. Be proud of your attempt to rid shopping addiction from your life. Never pity yourself or feel sorry; remember, as long as we are alive, there is always hope for change. If you are willing to change, be determined.

There are short-term and long-term effects associated with shopping addiction; it is important to be aware of its impact on you.

# Chapter 5:

# Medication & Therapy

In the previous chapter, you learned that overcoming shopping addiction begins with *awareness*. Once the problem is recognized, you can come up with a solution to beat the unwanted habit. The techniques on how to overcome addiction are up to you, but as many health professionals would agree, consulting a doctor is a good decision.

# The Five Plus Sides to Group Therapy

A great approach for the treatment of shopping addiction is registering for *group therapy*; being part of a group that meets regularly can boost your confidence level and cheer you on your journey. It makes you feel like you are a member of a team that's going to a similar destination. Apart from providing support, it reminds you that, in the process of overcoming a compulsive and budget-draining behavior, you are not alone.

According to Brown University's Warren Albert Medical School, a person who is suffering from addiction can find a higher level of comfort when surrounded by a group; the group, whether it is made up of fellow shopaholics or random individuals, can always encourage you to keep on going until complete recovery is achieved.

In comparison to a private therapy session, it provides you with a sense of safety; you are not on your own, since you have allies.

Let's have a look at the primary benefits of group therapy:

# A Gentle Personal Assessment

Group therapy allows you to speak up and share your own story. In this regard, it lets you feel free and in-control of your inner emotions that concern shopping addiction. You voice your take on your situation and have it received by an audience; if given permission, they can offer you their two cents' worth. This way, you can look at your current state, not just from your personal perspective, but from others', as well.

Moreover, the assessment on the story you share comes from people who are familiar with what it's like to be in your situation. Since they are from a group that knows where you are coming from and understand what you are going through, you learn to become responsive and use their comments, accordingly.

# Motivation & Empathy

With people who are aware of the process of beating addiction, you feel braver. Instead of dealing with too much anxiety from judgmental stares, you draw strength to express yourself and achieve progress as you try to overcome your issues.

Additionally, by listening to the successes and struggles that others have had to endure, you'll develop a sense of belief and empathy for yourself, as well as a wider perspective on how to approach your current situation.

## A Much-Needed Sounding Board

Since the group is there to listen to your random jokes, tales, and anything about your addiction, you find relief. With an audience, you enjoy the therapeutic effect of dealing with your current emotions. Instead of keeping them all bottled in, you put them out in the open; it reminds you that, despite being addicted to shopping, your worth as a person (who deserves to be heard) remains.

Truth be told, having someone listen to your story gives you a sense of validation. Coming to terms with the fact that you're suffering from an addiction means you've also discovered more fears, insecurities, and other mental concerns. To start rising above such issues, having a group that acknowledges your personal defeats and victories is a good strategy.

## Keeping Social Skills Intact

In a group session, you practice your social skills and detach yourself from isolation. Since you may have to interact regularly, you learn to be sensitive toward certain issues; instead of carelessly offending someone else, you learn to be polite and humble, by going out of your way to communicate effectively.

It reminds you that, just because you're a victim of addiction, it does not give you the right to make others feel under-appreciated, or allow you to become bitter at the factors (or people) that may have caused you to develop this habit.

## Cheaper Than Individual Therapy

The main reason group therapy is cheaper compared to individual therapy, is the overall costs are shared. You get to avail of savings, while getting much-needed help; the therapist in this case, benefits as well, since he/she receives higher compensation for his/her services.

Therefore, if you're a bit down when it comes to your budget, you can still seek treatment for shopping addiction. If you're worried that a group therapy session may not be as effective as an individual session, for the sole reason that the former costs less, you're quite wrong. Granted, you choose a therapist that is competent, qualified, has a roster of impressive group skills, chances are you're in good hands.

# The Role of Pharmacological Treatment

While there are no *specific medications* for curing shopping addiction, there are prescription medications available for shopaholics to help them deal with their problem; these are usually prescribed to manage the addictive behavior. The treatment addresses the issue that a shopaholic may likely be troubled mentally, first and foremost; the obsessive condition is merely a wall that conceals the hidden or the *real* problem.

As clinical psychologists suggest, the approach of treating shopping addiction should be focused on treating the *real condition*. The appropriate medications should then be taken. If you can get to the root of the problem, you can then proceed to finding a solution to the addiction. For instance, if the subject is suffering from depression, the method must, initially, revolve around the treatment of depression. If the depression is eliminated, so may the compulsive behavior.

However, although turning to medication is a practical method, it's recommended to consult a doctor, regarding the frequency or the dosage of the recommended drugs; make sure it does not get out of hand. To allow them to work wonders for your system, usage must be kept in moderation. The meds are supposed to help you, and their use shouldn't lead to *substance abuse*.

**The list of common conditions associated with shopping addiction are:**

Anxiety

Depression

Impulsivity

Indecisiveness

Low self-esteem

Perfectionism

Shame

## Cognitive Behavioral Therapy: Is It the Best Treatment Option?

A popular treatment option for shopaholics is *cognitive behavioral therapy*; it is a technique that combines two forms of therapies, namely cognitive therapy and, the more common, behavioral therapy. According to the National (US) Institute of Mental Health, its approach focuses on three things: a person's beliefs, thoughts, and actions. If these three things are kept in mind, a person with a shopping addiction can modify his/her mindset.

Moreover, cognitive behavioral therapy's approach is geared toward the awareness of a shopaholic's thoughts. In most cases, the reason shopaholics are clueless of their compulsive nature is due to the ignorance about their behavior. If enlightened that the proper way to act should be welcoming *adaptive* and *healthy* characteristics, they can successfully say goodbye to their addiction.

Like with pharmacological treatment, cognitive behavioral therapy promotes treatment of the severe mental condition. As statistics, based on surveys by clinical psychologists show, more than 50% of shopping addicts will no longer have a problem if they are in a sound mental state.

**The list of common disorders (associated with shopping addiction) that Cognitive Behavioral Therapy can treat are:**

Anger management

Anxiety

Bi-polar disorders

Depression

Eating disorders

Grief management

Schizophrenia

Sexual disorders

Sleep disorders

Substance abuse

Trauma

# Chapter Recap:

Group therapy sessions for the treatment of shopping addiction come with a number of advantages; if you want to maximize the benefits of therapy, attending sessions with your fellow shopaholics is something worth considering.

Pharmacological treatment has been proven effective. In essence, it works, since it targets the elimination of underlying mental conditions; in most cases, these mental health disorders are causing the addiction to get out of hand. Remember to consult with your doctor prior to consuming any pharmacological treatment methods.

Cognitive behavioral therapy is a popular treatment option to eliminate shopping addiction. Like most approaches meant for the management of a shopaholic's concerns, it stresses the importance of being in a sound mental state.

# Chapter 6:

# The "Conscious" Shopper

Now that we have gone over the mental part of your journey, as well the different medications and therapy programs to overcome shopping addiction, we will now look at some helpful techniques to halt your spending. Remember that shopping and buying things are not bad, but this habit should not come before more important obligations. The following are some simple, yet effective, ways of becoming the "conscious" shopper.

# The Seven Ways to Eliminate Shopping Addiction

These tips will help you take hold of your life, once more, and not succumb to addiction. Remember, the mind is a powerful force that can effectively dictate your actions. So, now that you have the mental perspective needed and the available resources to make it happen, it's time to set a goal and commit!

# Credit Card No More

The first thing you should do to avoid spending excessively is say goodbye to your credit card. Using your card to purchase things is so convenient that you will easily lose track of your spending; if you don't have a tool that grants you the chance to spend, you won't be tempted to shop. So, to start a new life, part ways with your credit card and don't let a small piece of plastic take control of your life ever again.

You may be thinking, *"But I want to build credit and earn points for other things in my life!"* Sure, there is no problem with that idea, but get one part of your life settled first; eliminate your compulsive behavior and worry about those things later. It doesn't take a lifetime to overcome shopping addiction, and you can work on building credit and earning points after you are sure your credit card isn't making your shopping decisions for you.

## Cash Is The Way To Go

As mentioned before, if you happen to need to buy anything, pay it in cash. Do not use any kind of installment options or use credit, as it will only pull you back into the quagmire of shopping addiction. If you do not have the money to buy it, save up for it. Even if it takes a while, save so you can pay for it in cash in the future. You will be surprised that you will actually feel even happier when you finally do purchase that thing you saved for.

By going this route, you'll notice that, because you actually have to go to the ATM to withdraw cash before purchasing, you'll make less poor buying decisions. This is because you're taking an extra step before you actually buy - making the action less compulsive and forcing you to put more thought into why you are going to withdraw the cash and hand it over to someone.

## Turn To A Friend

Next time you want to go to the mall to buy something, ask someone to accompany you. Never go shopping alone, as it is similar to an alcohol addict going to a bar alone. Have a dear friend or family member go with you every time you shop; this will help you refrain from buying excessively and going on spending sprees.

This simple, yet effective, tip will work especially well if you have taken the previous steps mentioned in the book and made sure to tell the person about your problem beforehand.

## Say NO to Temptations

Avoid making purchases online and refrain from letting your money go to home TV shopping networks. As usable (and entertaining) as their media showcases can be, find the courage to stop checking out their products. Remember, addiction only recurs when opportunities are present. So, always be wise and remove all triggers that will influence you to start spending again.

You might even want to remove your credit card information from any site online. You can adjust your browser settings so that you're forced to input the card's information every time you consider a purchase.

# Are Discounts Really Discounts?

Start to refrain from going to shops with discounts and promotions. This will only entice you to spend more to take advantage of the "cheaper" price. Steer clear of discounts, sales, promos, and the like. Always shop for what you need and do not spend a single dime on things that are not necessary in the next three months.

*The three-month rule* is very helpful for people trying to decide what is necessary. This will help with clothing, for example. If you haven't worn an item in three months, then you either need to donate that item or sell it (barring extremely sentimental items, like a wedding dress or letterman jacket). Likewise, if you are shopping for clothing at the store, do not purchase anything that you will not be wearing in the next three months.

If you are going to buy something to use/wear in the next three months, then replace it with something else in your possession, instead of adding it to your collection.

# A Shopping List On Standby

Disorganized spending can be just as bad as a spending addiction. This is why creating a shopping list, although seemingly trivial, is extremely necessary in order to keep track of one's budget. This is only practical.

Remember to always create small lists of things to buy every time you shop and never buy anything that is not on the list you made before you left the house.

## Money In The Hands Of Another

If you are really serious about finding a solution to your spending problem, then allowing others to handle your expenses and your money may be a good idea in the short-term. This is more of an extreme measure than the others, but if your problem is bad, you have nothing to lose (no pun intended).

You can either ask a close family member or a friend, or you can work with a person at your bank to get this done. There are many ways to set limits on your accounts, as well as monthly and weekly bank account reviews.

## Chapter Recap:

While the aforementioned tips and strategies may seem overly simple to those who have read on the topic of shopping addiction, the truth is that sticking to the fundamentals are the real key here.

There's no magical technique that will change your behaviors overnight. Use the information presented here as part of an overall game plan. For example, focus on adapting the mindset first, then enrolling in a weekly group therapy session, then implementing maybe one of these tips each week until you've incorporated all of them.

By just reading this information, you're not likely to see any significant changes in your behavior. IMPLEMENT.

# Chapter 7:

## Happy and Content - That's All That Matters

As we finally head towards the end of our journey, we already know what shopping addiction is, how it affects people, and its causes and possible cures. However, after many solutions have been given and a number of tips promoted, there is one sure solution that will prevent anyone from succumbing to shopping addiction: Be satisfied with the current possessions in your life and don't let material possessions define who you are.

As we mentioned, surface techniques you can use - the cure to overcoming the addiction for good - lie in overcoming the internal issues that trigger the compulsive behavior in the first place. If you combine the surface behaviors, mentioned in the last chapter, with the internal techniques in this chapter, you will get the maximum benefits.

## It Starts With Observation

Take a few weeks to become conscious of the triggers that cause you to get into a compulsive spending mindset. Maybe you have a compulsive skin picking issue or maybe you start to bite your nails. Focus on what behaviors you are doing throughout the day and what is causing them.

Many compulsive shoppers find that, when they are involved in a stressful situation with their significant other or their parents, shopping is the best outlet for them to release the built-up stress. What they are missing is, by fixing the root of the problem in their relationship(s), they can avoid shopping altogether.

If you find that family problems cause you to engage in compulsive behavior, focus on fixing the family problems, instead. If the family problems are too much to fix, try to limit the interactions you have with those people. You'll be amazed to find that, if you cut out most of the negative influences in your life, your negative compulsive behavior will usually lessen as well. The people with whom you interact with should be adding positivity and inspiring you to live a better life, not creating tension and making you feel anxious or uncomfortable.

# ieving Contentment

 Contentment is not the act of refraining from buying anything; it simply means not wanting more than what is already there. Being content makes luxuries impractical and spending for unnecessary things illogical. Once you feel content with your purchases and the people in your life, then you will have the advantage in your battle against shopping addiction.

So, be content; these two simple, yet powerful, words are the ultimate solution to overcoming shopping addiction. Without a sense of contentment, no one will ever be able to overcome spending addiction, because they are always in search of more possessions. However, happiness and contentment must be combined through the help of self-control in order to become effective.

The perfect middle ground is a person who buys nice things (that are high quality and will last long) when they need them, yet doesn't buy any items they do not need. By not letting material possessions define who you are as a person, you will notice that people may not notice you as much, but the people who do know you, will respect you much more.


This is because they are keeping you as a friend because of your character, instead of because of your possessions or the money you are willing to spend. Essentially, your true friends will still be attracted to you for the right reasons and those who liked you for the possessions you owned, will fade away, almost like a narrowing-down process.

# Self-Control Will Enter The Picture

Self-control is the ability to control one's own actions, and it is an important ingredient in addressing shopping addiction. Self-control can be developed by anyone; the only trick is to have determination and perseverance.

Once you are willing to perform an honest self-assessment, make a change, and make your life turn for the better, then you can follow these small, yet effective, tips that will help you live your dreams, free from the restricting chains of shopping addiction.

# The # 1 Goal

Remember, life is not only about today. The future and all the surprises it brings are still out there. So, just thinking about the future and the bigger picture, especially what overcoming your shopping addiction can do for your future life, is a great way to build self-control. Think about all the money that is going to waste if you break your word to yourself.

Do you want kids, someday? Do you want to retire at a certain age? Think about where you will be in the future and what situations you will find yourself in. By doing this, you will be more aware of how your short-term actions will affect your long-term opportunities. Maybe, if you want to send your children to college, that new dress or iPhone is not actually that important after all. What will your future self be glad that you did with your time and money, at this very moment?

## Mental Relaxation

Never stress out your mind in order to avoid rash and poor decisions. Always make sure you get adequate sleep and have outlets to vent your emotional stress, aside from spending. Meditation and deep breathing can be amazing steps to help you overcome shopping addiction, as well as other addictive behaviors.

Practicing even the most basic form of meditation forces a person to be more conscious of their behaviors, and it can really relax you if you are in a stressed out mental state. Doing this right when you feel the impulse to go spend will help you greatly.

By deep breathing four or five times when an impulse arises, your physiology actually changes and allows you to think more clearly. Try it next time you are in a situation where you feel like you want to give in and make a new purchase. Sit down, very still, close your eyes, and take four or five deep breaths while clearing your mind. Focus on your inhaling/exhaling and nothing else. You will be amazed at how you will lose that anxious feeling to spend.

## Let Go & Start Anew

Never judge yourself if you slip up on the path to overcoming this addiction; don't give in to personal frustrations. If you find yourself failing, put it into your mind that there is always a chance to bounce back and start over again; if the road to recovery isn't perfect, it doesn't mean it's no longer worth the pursuit.

It is useless to sulk and cry over spilt milk, so try to get it together and start anew. Once you have applied these methods of enhancing and maintaining self-control, overcoming addiction and becoming satisfied, happy, and content in life is a much easier process.

I can't emphasize enough how important it is to keep going, even if you just gave in to a huge shopping spree and feel horrible about your actions. If you went three weeks before buying something unnecessary, pat yourself on the back, because you are becoming more conscious, and you made some progress. Get back up and challenge yourself by going for four weeks this time. Look at this as a long-term process and remember why you are doing this in the first place.

**Chapter Recap:**

Always be present. Be grateful for the things you have, as well as the things you do not have. Remind yourself that it's alright not to have a lot of material possessions.

Don't take self-control for granted. Be decisive with your actions and make sure that, apart from giving you a hand in fighting shopping addiction, this skill will help you with your desired life in the long run.

Again, you are the one in control; remember to be in a sharp mental condition, so you are capable of thinking clearly. Learn to relax; over-thinking isn't helpful.

Focus on a long-term goal. Remind yourself that you need to beat shopping addiction, because it may have a drastic impact on your future and the decisions you'll be able to make down the road.

Learn to cut yourself some slack if you feel like you've failed along the process of overcoming addiction; try not to be too hard on yourself. Just learn to stay consistent. If you have to motivate and re-motivate yourself, by all means, do so.

# Conclusion

I worked hard on creating the best guide for "overcoming a shopping addiction" that I could. These are all the strategies and information that has worked for me, as well as others that I have talked to and researched. I guarantee that, if you stay consistent, they will work for you as well. Be optimistic about your current situation and make small progress each day!

If you've learned anything from this book, please take the time to share your thoughts by sending me a message, or even posting a review to Amazon.

Thank you and good luck in your journey!

Made in the USA
Monee, IL
12 January 2023